P9-CBD-301

The Treasury of Clean Country Jokes

The Treasury of Clean Country Jokes

Tal D. Bonham

BROADMAN PRESS
Nashville, Tennessee

© Copyright 1986 • Broadman Press
All rights reserved
4257-17
ISBN Number: 0-8054-5717-8
Dewey Decimal Classification: 808.87
Subject heading: JOKES
Library of Congress Catalog Number: 85-28045
Printed in the United States of America

Library of Congress Cataloging-in-Publication Data

Bonham, Tal D., 1934-
  The treasury of clean country jokes.

  1. Country life—Anecdotes, facetiae, satire, etc.
I. Title.
PN6231.C65B66   1986   818′.5402   85-28045
ISBN 0-8054-5717-8

Dedication

To the memory of *Grady Nutt* who believed that

"LAUGHTER IS THE HAND OF GOD ON THE SHOULDER OF A TROUBLED WORLD."

Acknowledgments

Without the encouragement and help of Chuck and Dottie Tommey, this little book could never have become a reality. Thanks, dear friends, for everything! And to your daughter, Sherri, a special word of thanks for pitching in at the last minute to help all of us when we almost missed the deadline. Charles and Janet, you were good sports about this project too.

Robert Larremore also helped to put it together and offered wise counsel. And, Faye, you helped all along the way. Thanks, darling.

Contents

Introduction

Her shrill "How DEE!" has echoed through countless concert halls and her dime-store hat, with the dangling price tag, is a trademark. Mrs. Henry Cannon, better known as Minnie Pearl, said in her autobiography, "Since religion was so much a part of my life as a child and since my childhood was so happy and full of life and joy, I associated the two."

I too have always associated religion with joy. Being a minister for over three decades, I have tried to find humor in many places. Some of the most humorous stories to be found are those which relate to the farm. Having been born and raised in the red hills of Western Oklahoma, I well remember attending the weekly auction sale on Saturday and hearing those homespun stories told by farmers and ranchers from far and near.

When I think of country humor, I think of clean humor. World-renowned country humorist, Jerry Clower, says, "Take my albums home and play them for your children and you won't be embarrassed." I like that! By the way, the same man, E. M. Bartlett, who wrote "Take an Old Cold Tater' and Wait" also wrote "Victory in Jesus"!

So here comes another volume of clean jokes and this time it is related to one of the best sources of humor in the world—the farm. I hope you enjoy it as much as I enjoyed putting it together.

Take it to church. Take it to the office. Take it to school. Take it into your home. Take it to the hospital and nursing home. Take it anywhere people like to laugh at good, clean humor.

TAL D. BONHAM

Accidents

Glenn: "How did you break your arm?"
Chester: "I fell out of a tree."
Glenn: "How far did you fall?"
Chester: "How far do you think? All the way to the ground!"

A city boy was hired as a ranch hand. He was assigned to take care of a bunch of mules. Knowing little about mules, he walked up behind one and slapped him on the backside. The mule kicked and knocked the boy unconscious.

Some of the other cowboys put the boy on a stretcher and started across the barnyard to a pickup truck to take him to the hospital. The faster they walked the more the stretcher swung in the air. Slowly the boy began to regain consciousness. He reached out his right hand and felt only air. He reached out his left hand and felt only air.

"Lord, help me," he prayed. "I haven't hit the ground yet."

Two boys were bragging about the accomplishments of their fathers.

"My old man was the first man to fly 10,000 feet with a stick in his hand," boasted one.

"Oh, he was a flyer?" asked his friend.

"No. The poolroom blew up."

A man and his wife went to the county fair. A pilot was taking people for an airplane ride for five dollars a person. The couple wanted to go, but the man thought the price was too high.

"Take us both for five dollars," he said.

The pilot wouldn't cut his price, but the man kept arguing.

"Tell you what," the pilot said at last. "You pay me ten dollars. If neither one of you says a word, I'll give your money back. It won't cost you a cent!"

The couple agreed and got into the plane. The pilot maneuvered his plane through every stunt he knew, but he didn't hear a sound. When he landed he turned to his customer and said, "You didn't say a word!"

"Nope," the man shook his head. "But I almost yelled when Ma fell out!"

Jack: "Heard about the terrible accident caused by a woman who backed her car out of the garage?"

Joe: "That's not such a bad accident."

Jack: "Oh, yes it was—her husband had backed it into the garage earlier."

"There's a short in my electric toothbrush," the woman screamed *frothily.*

The editor of a county newspaper was well known for confusing his copy. One day he received for publication an article about a wedding and a notice of an auction sale. He placed both pieces on either side of his typewriter and began to type:

"William Smith and Miss Lucy Anderson are to be disposed of at public auction at my farm one mile east of a beautiful cluster of roses on her gown before a background of farm implements too numerous to mention in the presence of seventy guests including two milk cows, six mules, and one bobsled. The pastor tied the nuptial knot with 200 feet of good hay wire.

"The bride wore a dark blue frock of green crepe with a full set of hames and traces, carrying in her hand several good bales of alfalfa hay.

Bridesmaids wore two nice, fat Duroc hogs weighing about 250 pounds each.

"The groom, attended by a 2 1/2-year-old Hereford bull, wore the conventional black.

"The bride entered upon the arm of her father, who was carrying a good double-barrel .12 gauge Remington shotgun now for sale cheap.

"The wedding march was played by a three horsepower gasoline engine on a good two-row corn cultivator with grass seed and corn drill plates.

"The bridle party left on one good John Deere tractor for an extended trip with terms to suit the purchaser. They will be home to their friends with one good baby buggy and a few other kitchen implements after date of sale to responsible parties and some fifty chickens."

The wife asked her husband, "Why didn't you give him half the road?"

The husband replied, "I would have if I could have figured out which half he wanted."

Judge: "The plowing contest was cancelled."

Contestant: "Why?"

Judge: "One fellow got the tractor stuck in reverse and unplowed five acres."

Ambition

"Farm" is a four-letter word meaning a chunk of land that, if you get up early enough mornings and work at it late enough nights, it'll make you rich—if you strike oil on it.

A tough sergeant was putting his new recruits through the drills. "Left face," he called, "right face, forward march, to the rear, march."

They went through this over and over again. Finally a tall, gangling farm boy sat down in disgust.

"What's the matter with you, Sonny Boy?" the sergeant roared.

"I'm not going to do another thing," the boy answered, "until you make up your mind what you want us to do."

Things won't change much in this automated world. The button that gets ahead will still be the one with the most push.

A candidate for Congress in a state that grew peas assured the voters that he would introduce a law which would stop England from shipping peas to the United States.

A stout gentleman, determined to lose weight during his stay on the farm, hustled to the store for a pair of overalls. He picked out a pair big enough for energetic exercise.

"Wait a minute," he said to the clerk, as a thought occurred to him. "Those fit me now, but I expect to lose a lot of weight. Maybe I'd better buy a smaller pair."

The clerk calmy went on wrapping up the overalls. "Mister," he said, "if you shrink as fast as those overalls will, you'll be doing pretty good!"

There was a farm hand who put iodine on his paycheck because he got a cut in pay. Ugh!

A man was walking through the woods and saw a bear. He ran as fast as he could, but the bear was getting closer every minute. Finally he saw a tree with a limb sticking out about twenty feet up in the air.

When he got home and was telling about his adventure, his wife asked, "Well, tell us, did you make it?"

"Not on the way up," he said, "but I caught that limb coming down!"

A farm boy got a white football for Christmas. He played with it awhile and then kicked it over into the neighbor's yard. The old rooster ran out, looked at it, and called the hens to see it.

"Now look here," the rooster said. "I don't want you girls to think I'm complaining, but I just want you to see what they are doing next door."

Did you hear about the man who shot an arrow into the air and missed?

Automobiles

A farmer was driving to town one morning with his wife. The weather was hot, and the windows were rolled up. "Honey," he said, "please open the windows."

"Are you crazy!" she exclaimed. "And let our neighbors driving in the next lane know that our car isn't air-conditioned?"

Dave: "Did you hear about the fellow who worked twelve hours a day at the muffler shop?"
Dan: "How did he feel after that?"
Dave: "He said it was *exhausting!*"

The teacher asked the class to name some of the benefits of the automotive age. After a silence, one boy spoke up, "Well, it stopped horse stealing."

A boy's parents wouldn't let him chew gum because they were afraid the sugar content would decay his teeth. So, as a very young lad he took up chewing little pieces of rubber cut from automobile tires.

On his twenty-first birthday, he had to have his teeth rotated and balanced.

Three Laws for Car Repairs

(1) Nothing minor ever happens to a car on the weekend.

(2) Nothing minor ever happens to a car on a trip.

(3) Nothing minor ever happens to a car.

Those little cars are a menace! Nowadays, when you cross a street, you have to look left, right, and down!

Question: "What is the definition of an autobiography?"

Answer: "The history of cars."

You know your car is getting old when they issue it upper and lower plates.

Baldness

Jared was about to get his first haircut. "I want my hair cut like my daddy's—with a hole on top," he shouted.

There are three ways for a man to wear his hair—parted, unparted, and departed.

A bald man wishes for one thing—dandruff!

Bald men can take comfort in the fact that they don't put marble tops on cheap tables. Unfortunately they are to be found on antiques, however.

Birds

Faye: "What happens when the price of duck feathers increases?"

Francis: "Then, down is up."

The young pigeon was just learning to fly. His mother tried to reassure him and said, "I'll tie one end of a piece of string around my leg and the other around your neck. If you get tired along the way, I'll help you."

The baby pigeon began to cry.

"What's the matter, my child?" asked the mother pigeon.

"Well, to be real honest with you, I don't want to be *pigeon-towed!*"

Eagle: Two strokes under the designated par in golf. As rare as the bird of the same name.

The mother hen was having trouble with her brood of chicks.

"If your daddy could see you now," she said. "He'd turn over in his gravy!"

"Why, that bird has no beak," the man said *impeccably.*

Jane: "I didn't know she'd taken up bird watching."

Jill: "Yes, she watches her husband like a hawk."

Question: "What do you call a bird with an artificial leg?"

Answer: "A lame duck."

A customer in a pet shop was contemplating the purchase of a parrot, which so far had given no sign of life other than to turn his head in her direction. Finally, she asked, "Does he talk?"

The salesman looked embarrassed. "Yes, ma'am, he talks, but he doesn't wish to be quoted."

Question: "Do you know how deep this river is?"

Answer: "It can't be that deep. It's only up to that duck's stomach."

A hog buyer saw a drove of hogs, large but lean, acting quite peculiarly. They would run in a bunch to one part of the field, stay there a few minutes, then dash to a different place. He mentioned their peculiar nervousness to the farmer.

The farmer, in a hoarse whisper, explained that he had always called the hogs to feed them, but when he took cold and lost his voice, he pounded on the fence with a stick to bring them.

"Now," he said, "the crazy woodpeckers are running those hogs to death."

Bragging

A priest was listening to a young man confess his sins. He stopped him and said, "Wait a minute, young man, you aren't confessing—you're bragging!"

A hawk, a lion, and a skunk were arguing over who was the most feared animal in the jungle.

The hawk said, "I am feared more than any animal in the jungle, because I attack from above and see things that no one else can see!"

The lion said, "I am the strongest animal in the jungle and no one can doubt it!"

The skunk said, "I can put up a stink that will scare man or beast out of the jungle!"

As the three were engrossed in the discussion, a grizzly bear came along and swallowed them all—Hawk, Lion, and Stinker!

Flattery: Phony express.

Braggart: A fellow whose mouth saves you the trouble of finding out for yourself how wonderful he is.

You don't feel like bragging when at the super-market, the automatic door opens for everyone but you.

A man was boasting of his ancient lineage and his distinguished ancestors who had come over on the Mayflower. The farmer, listening patiently, finally said, "That's too bad, friend, because in my business we say: 'The older the seed, the worse the crop.'"

Two boys and a girl were boasting about their fathers.

"My father bathes twice a week," said the first boy.

"That's nothing," said the girl. "My father bathes three times a week."

"Oh, yeah?" said the second boy, "my dad keeps himself so clean he never has to take a bath!"

A braggart thought he was so great because his friends were throwing a party in his honor. But nobody would tell him where it was to be held.

Boast not too loudly of your open mind, lest you be judged as having holes in your head.

A Texan was bragging on a bus trip in Michigan. None of his listeners had ever visited Texas, and he wanted to impress them with its greatness.

"You can enter Texas in the morning, travel all day, go to sleep, and when you wake up the next morning, you will still be in Texas," stated the Texan.

The others didn't seem to be impressed, so he decided to stretch things a bit: "And you can travel all that day, too, and you will still be in Texas."

One of his listeners leaned forward and said: "We've got buses like that right here in Michigan, too."

She had two daughters, both married, and she bragged on both of her sons-in-law.

"They both want me to visit at the same time," she said. "The one in the East wants me in the West, and the one in the West wants me in the East."

A veteran master sergeant was having trouble with a very confident teenage recruit. Although the youngster bragged a lot, he had a disconcerting knack of making good his boasts.

As they marched to the rifle range, he announced that he was the best shot in the rookie unit—and lived up to it by outshooting the other recruits. That night in the barracks, everyone suffered through his detailed account of how he "set a new range record."

Turning to his sergeant, the boastful youngster remarked: "Bet you didn't shoot that well when you first joined up, Sarge."

After a pause, the sergeant replied: "No, son, I didn't. But when I first shot, there was somebody shooting back at me."

Bill: "My daddy has a sword of Washington and a hat of Lincoln."

Joe: "My father has an Adam's apple."

A "self-made man" refused to go to church because he said, "That pastor can't tell me anything in a sermon that I don't already know." However, a friend persuaded him to go, and asked him later if he had learned anything at church.

"Well, yes," he said, "I learned that Sodom and Gomorrah were two cities. I always thought they were man and wife like Dan and Beersheba."

Bravery

A high percentage of accidents happen in the kitchen but people have to eat them.

The preacher called on a church family that had recently bought a bulldog. The dog was in the yard. The dog looked mean so the preacher stopped at the gate. The lady came to the door and said: "Come on in."

"Will the dog bite?" the preacher asked.

"I don't know, that's what we want to find out," the lady answered.

Son: "Say, Dad, that apple I just ate had a worm in it, and I ate that too."

Dad: "Wait! Here, drink this water and wash it down."

Son: "Nah, let him walk down!"

"How do you know this dog is a bloodhound?" asked the suspicious lady of the pet shop owner.

"Bleed a little for the lady," he ordered the dog.

Don't be afraid to make your mark in the world,

even though you're sure someone will use an eraser on it.

On a winter day after a large snow, the pastor went for a walk. At one point, he slipped and fell down in the snow. A little girl came up and asked if she could help him.

"You're too little," the pastor said.

She replied, "I've helped my daddy up many times when he was drunker than you are."

Church

A country church had the following sign over the main door of the church: "You are not too bad to come in. You are not too good to stay out."

A Sunday School teacher was reviewing her pupils on a unit of lessons. She placed an apple on the table.

"This is my apple," she said. "If you see someone take it, what Bible verse does it bring to mind?"

"Thou shalt not steal," a wise pupil answered promptly.

"That's good. Now if you see two boys fighting, what verse comes to you?"

"Be ye kind one to another," a pupil answered.

Now the teacher wanted to remind the pupils about being kind to animals. "If these boys were fighting over a cat," she said, "and one boy was pulling the cat's front legs and the other the cat's tail, what verse would that remind you of?"

All of the pupils thought a moment. Finally one raised his hand.

"What God hath joined together, let not man put asunder!" he answered.

In its endeavor to make money for a new organ, a church decided to dedicate a hymn to each person who contributed ten dollars. One lady gave thirty dollars. The pastor commended her and asked her which hymns she wanted.

Using her finger to point, the unmarried matron said, "I'll take him and him and him."

Four cows leaped out of a passing truck and fled through traffic right into a church. Some excitement ensued, but no damage.

"It just shows you," cracked the pastor, "that we are a church with an open door."

The minister delivered a sermon in ten minutes, about half the normal time. He explained, "I regret to inform you that my dog who is very fond of eating paper ate that portion of my sermon which I have not delivered this morning."

After the service, a visitor from another church shook hands with the preacher and said, "Pastor, if that dog of yours has any pups, I want to get one to give to my minister."

A minister preached a series of sermons on "All the Sins of Mankind." People kept calling him to get the list to see if they had missed anything.

A farmer attended his first church convention. After the convention was over, his pastor asked him to evaluate it.

"It was all right, but I didn't understand all that discussion about how to get people to come to church. When I go to a farmer's convention, I never hear them discussing how to get the cows to come to the barn. They know that if you put plenty of good hay in the feeder, the cows will come to get it."

Courting

Roses are red,
Violets are blue;
Orchids are $18.95!
Will dandelions do?

An ad in a country newspaper read: "Handsome and intelligent farmer wishes to meet a young woman who owns a tractor. Please write soon and enclose a picture of the tractor."

Young man to girl friend: "I wouldn't change a thing about you—but your name."

"Isn't it wonderful," a young lady said to her friend, "God made almost the same number of men as he did women?"

"Yes," her friend replied, "a man for every woman and a woman for every man."

"That's something you can't improve on, isn't it?" the young lady asked.

"Oh, I don't want to improve on it," her friend said, "I just want to get in on it."

"You sit in the park with a nice girl. What do you do?"

"I buy some popcorn."

"No, no, no, you put your arm around her and your lips to her lips. Then what do you do?"

"I take back my popcorn."

A couple had dated for several years. Everytime he tried to ask her to marry him, he became speechless. He finally determined to find the nerve to ask her.

On a beautiful Sunday afternoon he drove her out to the cemetery. They walked along the paths until they came to a lot with space for two graves. Looking down, he gathered all his courage.

"I bought this lot yesterday," he said. "How would you like to be buried here, side by side?"

"All right, I guess," she answered. "But I'd a whole lot rather get married and live together awhile."

Cows, Bulls

Farmer: That new man I hired yesterday doesn't know much about farming.

Wife: Why do you say that?

Farmer: He saw some milk cans behind the barn and ran to me shouting he'd found a cow's nest.

Two men were crossing a ranch pasture when a bull started after them. They dashed across the pasture until they came to one small tree. One man climbed into the tree. His companion jumped into a hole near the tree.

The bull charged by, barely missing the tree and the hole. Suddenly the bull stopped, pawed the ground, and snorted. About this time the man in the hole jumped up. The bull wheeled about and charged once more, flattening the man to the ground.

"Why didn't you stay in the hole?" the other man yelled from the tree. "Get back in there!"

His friend yelled back, "There's a bear in the hole!"

Request: "Please tell me how long cows should be milked."

The obvious answer: "Five or ten minutes."

The wise guy's answer: "The same as short ones."

Farmer: "We use a very special milk pail with our electric milking machines."
City slicker: "Why?"
Farmer: "Because one good urn deserves an udder."

Cowboys

A preacher who went from ranch to ranch preaching to the cowboys rode up to a ranch and found only one man.

"Where is everybody?" the preacher asked. "I've come out here to preach."

"We didn't know you was comin'," the cowhand explained. "I'm the only one here, but if I went out to feed the cows and only one showed up, I would feed that one. Go ahead and preach if you want to."

Thinking the old cowboy was hungry to hear the gospel, he preached for more than two hours. When he finished, he laid his hand on the cowhand's shoulder.

"How did you like that sermon?" he asked.

"All right," the cow-puncher shrugged.

The preacher wasn't satisfied. "That's no answer," he said. "Now tell me, how did you like it?"

"Well, sir," the cowboy drawled, "if I come out here with a whole truckload of feed, and didn't find but one cow, I wouldn't feed it a whole load!"

Don: "Dr. Dan opened up his dental office in a city populated by many cowboys."

Julie: "What do they call him?"

Don: "The gumslinger."

During a terrible rainstorm, a stranger remarked to a teenage cowboy, "Awful weather! Lots of rain! Reminds me of the flood!"

"The what?" asked the young cowboy.

"The Flood—Noah—the Ark—Mount Ararat," the stranger explained.

The cowboy shook his head, "I ain't seen the mornin' paper yet."

An old ranchhand had gone to the city to sell cattle. While he was there he decided to buy himself some clothes. The salesman was the "high-pressure" type who kept urging him to buy more.

"How about some nightshirts?" he asked.

"Don't get smart with me, young man," the old rancher said angrily. "When night comes, I go to bed."

Dogs, Cats

A tourist taking pictures asked the farmer, "How come your dog has such a short nose?" The farmer replied, "He chases parked cars!"

"They are training dogs to sniff watermelons for pesticides like the ones that sniff luggage for drugs."
"What do they call them?"
"Melon Collies!"

Question: Where can you buy a metal dog leash?
Answer: In a chain store.

A boy's mother told him, "You mustn't pull the cat's tail like that."
"I'm only holding it, Mom," he said. "The cat is pulling."

You know you need to go on a diet when you step on your dog and it dies.

A dog veterinarian has a barking lot near his office.

A hunter was talking to a group of his friends about the great hunting dog he had and all about its wonderful skills. Then as an afterthought, he added, "Of course, he's got one drawback—he likes to follow a track backward!"

Sherri: "You know, I'm kind of worried. The guy I've been dating has invited me over for dinner and he asked me to pick up some dog food on the way over."
Janet: "What's so strange about that?"
Sherri: "He doesn't have a dog!"

Tom: What's the difference between a cat and a frog?
Linda: A cat has only nine lives—a frog croaks every minute. Eeek!

Sign near a dog hospital—"HOSPITAL ZONE —NO BARKING!"

A lady was bitten by a dog with rabies. Her

minister, knowing hydrophobia to be an incurable disease, called on her and tactfully suggested that she write her will before the vicious disease took its toll. She agreed and began writing while he waited. She wrote and wrote and wrote. Finally, the preacher inquired about it.

"Rather a long will, isn't it?"

"Who's writing a will? This is a list of the people I intend to bite."

Jason: Why did Mama Flea look so sad?

Jared: Because all her children were going to the dogs.

A man appeared in a newspaper office to place an ad offering a large reward for the return of his wife's cat.

"That's an awfully high price for a cat," the clerk suggested.

"Not for this one," said the man. "He drowned."

My dog is a bit vicious. If he likes you he doesn't lick your hand; he lets you keep it.

Wife: "Feed the dog."

Husband: "He just ate. I can still smell the mailman on his breath."

Boy to friend: "My dog doesn't have a tail."
Friend: "How do you know when he's happy?"
Boy: "He stops biting me."

Dan: "My dog doesn't have a nose."
Dave: "How does he smell?"
Dan: "Terrible."

Cats do not pose for calendars . . .
. . . real cats couldn't care less what day it is
. . . or what month . . . or even what year.
Real cats do not sing in the bath.
The only thing a real cat hates more than opera is being immersed in water.

Family

A salesman was walking along a country road and stopped to chat with a farmer who was mowing a hay field. He asked the farmer, "And what does your son do?"

"He's a boot black up in the city."

"Ah, I see," exclaimed the witty fellow. "So you make hay while the son shines!"

Most of us don't have any use for the advice of our parents until we start raising families of our own.

Doctor: "I don't like the way your wife looks!"
Farmer: "I ain't too crazy about her looks either, but she's good at milking, wood cuttin', and right good to me and the kids!"

Did you hear about the young farmer who took his expectant wife to the grocery store because he heard that they had free deliveries? Yeeek!

Mother: "I never told lies when I was a child."
Daughter: "When did you begin?"

The country parson rode his horse to visit a very isolated, rural home. He saw only a young girl outside, so he asked for her father.

"Cain't speak to him," she explained. "Pap's in the penitentiary."

"Well then, how about your mother?"

"She's been took to the hospital. She was seein' things."

"Ah, sad," the minister shook his head. "But perhaps I could speak with your brother."

"Oh, my brother's away at college."

The preacher brightened up. "How nice! What is he studying?"

"He ain't studyin' nuthin'," said the girl. "They're studyin' him."

A farmer's six-year-old rushed into his mother's bedroom at two in the morning and asked her to tell him a story.

"Just wait a little while, honey," she said. "Your father will come home and tell us both one."

The farmer's wife had twin daughters. When the first girl was born, they named her "Kate." When the second one was born a few minutes later, they named her "Duplikate."

A young man told his father that he was leaving the hills. "I'm looking for adventure, excitement, and beautiful women," said the young man to his father. "Don't try to stop me. I'm on my way."

"Who's trying to stop you?" yelled his father. "I'm going with you."

It was his first day back on the job after his vacation.

"How did you enjoy your trip?" asked the fellow worker.

"Well," sighed the weary traveler, "have you ever spent a week in a station wagon with those you thought you loved best?"

Fishermen

Two friends were avid fishermen. One day, after catching many fish, one came upon the other who had caught none.

"Greetings," said the first with his stringer full of fish. "There sure are plenty of fish in this lake."

The other sadly replied, "Yes, and I'm the one who left them there!"

On a job application blank was the question, "Have you ever been arrested for fishing in a posted lake?" The applicant put down "No."

The next question was "Why?"

The applicant wrote, "Never been caught."

The little boy was late for Sunday School. His teacher, seeing him slip in, detained him and asked his reason for being late. The boy shuffled his feet uncertainly for a moment, then blurted out, "I started out to go fishing this morning and my dad wouldn't let me."

The teacher beamed broadly. "A wise father," he said. "He was quite right not to let you go fishing on a Sunday.

The little boy nodded. "Yes, he said there wasn't enough bait for the two of us!"

Mother to Son: "Why don't you take your little sister with you when you go fishing today?"

"No," said the son. "Last time she tagged along I didn't catch a fish."

"I'm sure she'll be quiet this time," said the mother.

"It wasn't the noise," said the youngster. "She ate the bait."

Fish should be selected on the basis of one's profession, as follows:

Carpenter - Sawfish.
Shoemaker - Sole.
Jazz musician - Drum.
Policeman - Starfish.
Sea Captain - Skipper.
Lawyer - Shark.
Miser - Goldfish.

A six-year-old boy went fishing for the first time with his father. He was rather bored by the whole event so, after about an hour, he took a walk in the woods.

A few minutes later, his father heard a strange cry. He found a man hopping around on one foot, caressing the other foot and groaning painfully.

"What happened?" asked the father.

His six-year-old son spoke up and said, "I guess

it's my fault, Dad. This man told me he hadn't had a bite all morning—so I bit him!"

An old fisherman sat on the river bank, obviously awaiting a nibble though the fishing season had not officially opened. The game warden stood behind him quietly for several minutes.

"You a game warden?" the fisherman asked.

"Yep."

Unruffled, the old man began to move the fishing pole from side to side. Finally, he lifted the line out of the water.

"Just teaching him how to swim," he said, pointing to the minnow wiggling on the end of the line.

Food

Hamburger:
A steak that didn't pass its physical.

You know you need to go on a diet when your wife tells you that if you don't lose weight she's going to kick you out of the house (and she's already hired the bulldozer).

A country preacher was invited to a home for lunch following the morning service. It was the home of a very large family. After the preacher finished with a rather lengthy prayer, the lady asked him, "Now, what will you have for dessert?"

Waitress: "How did you find the meat, sir?"
Customer: "I just lifted up a potato chip, and there it was."

A minister made his regular rounds at the local nursing home. One of his favorite people, a ninety-year-old saint, was out of her room at the time.

While he sat and waited on her, he munched on a bowl of peanuts sitting by her bedside.

Aunt Ella finally entered the room and apologized for being out when he arrived. The minister said, "Oh, Aunt Ella, that's all right. I enjoyed sitting here."

Then, he glanced over at the bowl of peanuts and noticed that he had eaten the very last one.

Upon apologizing to Aunt Ella for eating all of her peanuts, she comforted him by saying, "Oh, pastor, don't worry about that. I really don't eat peanuts anyway. My teeth are so bad that I just suck the chocolate off of them and leave them there in that bowl."

Tina: "How do you know when someone likes to eat bread?"

Ted: "They seem to fall in loaf with it." Yippee!

A wife woke up her husband, excitedly saying: "Wake up. There's a burglar in the kitchen, and he's eating up the rest of the pie we had for dinner."

Her husband rolled over and said, "Go back to sleep. I'll bury him in the morning."

"Why don't you wash your face? I can see what you had for breakfast this morning."

"Okay, smart aleck. What did I have?"

"Pizza!"

"Wrong, I had that yesterday!"

Methuselah

Methuselah ate what he found on his plate
And never, as people do now,
Did he note the amount of the calorie count;
He ate it because it was chow.
He wasn't disturbed as at dinner he sat,
Devouring a roast or a pie,
To think it was lacking in granular fat
Or a couple of vitamins shy.
He cheerfully chewed each species of food,
Unmindful of troubles or fears
Lest his health might be hurt
By some fancy dessert,
And lived almost a thousand years.

Newlyweds: "We just bought our first coffee percolator!"

Friend: "Well, that's grounds for celebration!"

A teenager told the clerk at a garden and nursery store, "My mother wants a powder that kills beetles, weeds, and spinach."

Dick: "Do you know how you ship vegetables?"
Dan: "By *parsley* post."

Forty extra pounds can make you feel better if you see it on someone you almost married.

The best way to raise strawberries—with a spoon.

A little girl was left to fix lunch. When her mother returned with a friend, she noticed that the tea had already been strained.

"Did you find the tea strainer?" asked the mother.

"No, Mother, I couldn't, so I used the fly swatter," replied the little girl.

Her mother nearly fainted, so the little girl hastily added, "Don't get excited, Mother. I used the old one."

I'm not counting calories and I've got the figure to prove it.

"I was not born; I was baked in an oven," the strange man declared *gingerly*.

The boy was sent by his mother to buy a 95-cent loaf of rye bread at the corner bakery. While the clerk was putting the bread into a bag, the boy noticed that the loaf was not very large.

"Isn't that a small loaf of bread for 95 cents?" he asked.

"You'll have less to carry," said the clerk.

The boy put two quarters on the counter.

"You are 45-cents short," said the clerk.

"That's right," replied the boy. "You'll have less to count."

The Belt Diet—Take your belt and tie it around the refrigerator.

I can't find the bluebird of happiness because of too many swallows.

Question: How do you know when you have a weight problem?

Answer: When someone criticizes you for being overweight and all you can do is turn the other chin.

Havoc

The greatest surprise on Christmas morning—
"Batteries not included."

A farmer was in the post office when suddenly
his neighbor came rushing in and shouted, "I
think somebody's a stealin' yore pickup!"

The farmer ran out but then returned right
away. "Did you stop him?" asked his neighbor.

"Naw, he was too fast," said the farmer, "but
I got his license plate number."

"Pilot to control tower! Pilot to control tower!"
came the booming voice of the crop duster. "I'm
coming in! Please give instructions!"

"Control tower to pilot," came the answer. "All
right, but why are you yelling so loud?"

"I've got to," shouted the crop duster. "I don't
have a radio!"

The farmer had never seen a motorcycle. While
out walking with his daughter one day one came
roaring down the road.

"Shoot, Pa, shoot!" exclaimed his daughter.

The farmer picked up his rifle and shot five times.

"Did you kill it, Pa?" asked the daughter.

"Naw," said the farmer, "it's still growlin'. But I made it let go of the man it was carryin'."

A couple of musicians were discussing a mutual friend. "It was really just awful about Clarence," said the first.

"Oh, what happened?"

"He was playing in last night's concert when his toupee fell into his tuba!"

"I can see why he might be embarrassed, but why was it so awful?"

"Because in one of the reviews this morning, it said Clarence spent the entire concert blowing his top!"

Hobos

Hobo: A *roads scholar.*

Farmer: "For this job we want someone who is responsible."

Hobo: "That's for me. Everywhere I've worked, whenever something went wrong, I was responsible."

A hobo came knocking on doors one day looking for any kind of odd jobs. He came up to this very large house in the country and asked if there was anything he could do.

"Sure, you can paint our porch. You'll find all the brushes and paint you'll need out in the garage. Will fifty bucks be okay?"

The hobo said, "Fifty bucks! That's great!"

So he went off toward the garage, and his new employer went in the house to tell his wife he had found someone to paint the porch.

About thirty minutes later there was a knock on the front door. The hobo was standing there with paint speckles all over him. "I'm all done!" he announced. "And by the way, it wasn't a Porche —it was a Ferrari!"

Hobo: Mister, can you spare a hundred dollars for a cup of coffee?

Stranger: A hundred dollars! How many people do you think are going to give you a hundred dollars?

Hobo: Well, if only three or four did, I could take a month's vacation.

A southern tomato grower hired a hobo to grade his tomatoes.

"All you have to do is go through these tomatoes and put the large ones in that bin over there. If the tomatoes are small, put them in that other bin over here."

After a half hour, the fellow came to his employer and announced nervously that he was quitting.

"But it's not hard work," the grower protested.

"Oh no, the work is easy enough, but I can't stand making all those decisions."

A ragged, hungry hobo stopped a well-dressed rich man on the street and asked him for food money. "I'll do better than that," said the rich man, "come into the bar and I'll buy you a drink."

"Thank you, sir," said the beggar, "I'm not a drinking man."

"Well, then have a cigar," offered the rich man.

"No, thanks, I don't smoke."

"Okay," said the rich man. "I'll make a bet for you on a horse that's absolutely guaranteed to win, and you'll collect enough cash for plenty of food and a new suit besides."

"Please no," said the hobo. "I only need a bite —just a bite."

"Well, then," said the rich man, "How would you like to come home with me to dinner? I want my wife to see for herself what happens to a guy who doesn't smoke, drink, or gamble."

Horses, Mules

Did you hear about the university that had to do away with Driver's Ed?

The mule died.

A country parson had three horses which he named "High Church," "Low Church," and "Broad Church."

He said, "The first is always on his knees, the second never prays, and you never know what the other one will do next."

At times the only thing you get right from the horse's mouth is the horse's laugh.

Two farmer friends met, and the first farmer asked, "Didn't your horse have this disease that's going around?"

"Sure did, had it bad," replied the friend.

"What did you do for him?" asked the first farmer.

"I dosed him good with a half-pint of linseed oil, a tablespoonful of turpentine, and three table-spoons of castor oil."

A few days later the two farmers met again.

"Didn't you tell me you gave your horse a half-pint of linseed oil, a tablespoonful of turpentine, and three tablespoons of castor oil?" the first farmer asked.

"Sure did!"

"I thought that was what you said. But when I gave it to my horse he died."

"So did mine!"

A pastor was invited to lunch one day at the home of a well-to-do church member. To the pastor's surprise and that of his host, there was no knife, fork, or spoon at the pastor's plate.

The wife asked her young daughter why she had not placed any silverware at the pastor's place.

"Oh, he doesn't need any," she answered. "Daddy says he eats like a horse!"

Horse sense is hardly enough in this world even for horses.

Two horses were discussing a very important race. "I've got to win!" said the first horse.

"Why? If you win it's just more money for your owner."

"Neigh, neigh," said the first horse, "my owner

promised me thirty extra bales of hay if we win this race. I've just got to win!"

"Thirty bales of hay!" exclaimed the other horse. "Hay. That ain't money!"

An IRS agent said to a farmer riding in a mule cart, "We need to talk about the twenty-five cents a mile deduction you took!"

A farmer fell and broke his hip while he was plowing, and his horse galloped five miles to the nearest town and returned carrying a doctor on his back.

"Pretty smart horse," a friend observed later.

"Well, not really so smart," the farmer said. "The doctor he brought back was a veterinarian."

Lawyer in carriage: "What's wrong, driver?"

Driver: "The horses are running away, Sir. Can't control them."

Lawyer: "Well, if you can't stop 'em, then run 'em into something cheap!"

A mild-mannered, conservative minister accepted the call to a church in a community where many residents bred and raced horses.

A few weeks later he was asked to have the congregation pray for May Rose. Willingly and gladly, he did so for three weeks. On the fourth Sunday the church member that had requested prayer informed the minister that the prayers were no longer necessary.

"Why?" asked the good minister with an anxious look. "Did she die?"

"Oh, no," replied the church member, "she won her race."

Horse sense dwells in a stable mind.

Question: "What do you call a cross between a fox and a mule?"

Answer: "A fool."

An Army captain told some new recruits to take a mule and "have him shod." After awhile the soldiers returned. Two of them had rifles, and the others were carrying shovels.

"Did you get the mule shod?" the captain asked.

The soldiers looked at one another. "Did you say *shod?*" they all asked in unison.

Hotels, Motels

One teenager to another: "Did you hear about the haunted motel?"

"No, what about it?"

"It had twenty scream doors."

A farmer took his wife to a large city on their wedding anniversary so they could stay overnight in a hotel for the first time in their lives.

When the bellboy showed them to their room, a look of disappointment came over the wife's face.

"What's the matter?" the farmer asked.

The wife pointed at the twin beds and said, "When you said we were going to stay in a hotel, I didn't think we'd have to share a room with somebody else."

Epitaph on a motel manager's tombstone: "Do Not Disturb."

Dave: "They say there are very few hotel telephones in China."

Dan: "I wonder why."

Dave: "Well, stupid, you ought to know why—

there are too many people named Wing and Wong."

Dan: "Oh, I guess that explains it—they're afraid too many people will wing the wong number!"

The elderly lady from the country, checking into a hotel, said to the bellman, "I refuse to take a tiny room like this with no windows and no bed in it. You can't treat me like a fool just because I don't travel much. I'm going to complain to the manager."

"Madam," the bellman said. "This isn't your room. This is the elevator."

In order to conserve energy, the motel erected the following sign in every room: "Please turn off the lights when not using them. Thanks a watt!"

Husbands, Wives

A girl engaged to be married said, "But father, I don't want to leave mother!"

Said he, "I understand, but don't let me stand in the way of your happiness. Take your mother with you!"

A happy marriage exists when the couple is as deeply in love as in debt!

A husband said to his wife, "Now tomorrow why don't you take Junior to the zoo?"

"What do you mean, *take* him?" responded his wife. "If they want him, they can come and get him."

"I feel real generous today," a woman told a friend. "I started the day out by giving a dollar to a bum."

"You gave a bum a whole dollar?" her friend asked. "What did your husband say?"

"Thanks, honey!" replied the woman.

A farmer's wife applying for a charge account

for the first time was asked about her husband's average income.

"Usually around midnight," she replied.

"When my wife and I get into an argument she becomes historical!"

"You mean hysterical, don't you?" asked his friend.

"No, I mean historical—she keeps bringing up the past!"

A woman went to her pastor with her troubles.

"I'm afraid my husband doesn't love me anymore," she said.

"You mustn't jump at conclusions," the pastor reassured her.

"But I can't help being uneasy," she insisted.

"Why do you think your husband doesn't love you anymore?"

"He's been gone five years, and I haven't heard a word from him."

Sometimes a wife drives a man to distinction.

Linda: "You were more gallant when I was a gal."

Wendell: "You were more buoyant when I was a boy."

A woman was reporting her missing husband to the police—"He's short . . . bald-headed . . . wears false teeth . . . chews tobacco, and the juice is always running down his chin . . . on second thought, officer . . . just forget the whole thing!"

Freda: "Do you know what happens every time I asked my husband to plant a garden?"
Faye: "No, what?"
Freda: "Well, the first thing he digs up is an excuse!"

"For months," said a busy country-club member, "I couldn't imagine where my husband spent his evenings."

"And then what happened?" breathlessly asked her friend.

"Well," she said, "one evening I went home, and there he was."

A couple, married for fifty years, always remembered each other's birthdays. Then one year her birthday came along, and she must have forgotten it herself because she didn't do a thing to jog his memory.

That night he was reading the paper and saw a story about a big birthday party. Suddenly he remembered her birthday. He started thinking about all their years together, the heartaches and struggles they'd been through, and what a fine wife she'd been.

She'd grown rather hard of hearing in the last few years so he leaned toward her and yelled, "Wife, I'm proud of you."

She sat up straight in her chair. "That's nothing!" she said. "I'm tired of you too!"

Every man needs a wife because there are a number of things that go wrong that one can't blame on the government.

The wife who is a backseat driver is no worse than the husband who cooks from the dining room table.

Illness

"Where are you going?" asked his sister as the Saturday morning cartoons came on T.V.

"Outside," he replied

"Why?"

"Because, Mickey Mouse gives me Disney spells!"

"Morbus Sabbaticus" is a disease peculiar to church members. Here are some of its symptoms:

1. It never interferes with the appetite.

2. It never lasts more than twenty-four hours at a time.

3. No physician is ever called.

4. It is contagious.

The attack usually comes on suddenly every Sunday. No ill effects are felt on Saturday night, and the patient awakes as usual, feeling fine. He eats a hearty breakfast. About 9 AM the attack comes on, and it lasts until around noon.

In the afternoon the patient is much improved. He is able to take a ride, read the Sunday newspaper, or watch a football game. The patient eats a hearty supper, but the attack comes on again and lasts through the evening. The patient is able to go to work Monday—as usual.

"You have diabetes," the doctor said *sweetly.*

Down in the country, it's customary to measure medicine with whatever's handy. Not long ago, a small-town doctor met the husband of one of his patients on the street.

"How's your wife, Jake?" he asked. "Did you give her that sleeping powder as I suggested? Just as much as you could get on a quarter?"

"Well, Doc," answered Jake. "I didn't have a quarter, so I gave her what I could get on five nickels. That was a week ago and she's still asleep."

Question: What does a doctor do when you ask him to shave your bill?
Answer: He goes into a lather.

A man with a terrible cold went to his doctor. After the examination the doctor said, "You've got an awful cold."

"I know it, Doc, that's why I came to see you."

The doctor said, "You go home, take off your shoes and your shirt, go out on the north side of the house, and stand in the snow for an hour and a half."

"Doc," said the man, "that will give me pneumonia."

The doctor said, "I know. You see, I know how to cure pneumonia, but I don't know how to cure a cold."

A man walked into a store and said, "I'd like some DDT, please."

"Sure," came the response, "but, how do you spell it?"

Laziness

A lazy fellow wrote out a prayer and tacked it on the ceiling over his bed. When he fell in bed at night, he would point to the ceiling and fall asleep.

Some people are like blisters; they never show up until after the work is done.

A college student went into the men's section of a department store and asked for seven pairs of underwear. The clerk asked him, "Why just seven?"

"For Monday, Tuesday, Wednesday, Thursday, Friday, Saturday, and Sunday," he replied.

The next day another college student came in and also asked for seven pairs of underwear also for Monday, Tuesday, Wednesday, etc. Later, another fellow came in and asked for some underwear.

The clerk said, "Sure, and I bet you want seven pairs."

"Nope," came the reply, "I want twelve."

"Twelve?" said the clerk.

"Yes, twelve—January, February, March, April, May, June, July, August, September, October, November, and December."

He had the reputation of being the laziest man in town. During a revival meeting he made a profession of faith and joined the church. Everyone wondered what changes they would see in the new convert. The next Sunday the pastor called on him for prayer.

"Lord, use me," he prayed fervently. "Use me in an advisory capacity."

An old mountaineer and his son were sitting in front of the fire as they whittled.

After a long silence, the father said, "Son, step outside and see if it's raining."

Without looking up, the son answered, "Aw, Pa, why don't we just call in the dog and see if he's wet?"

A fellow was so lazy that he wouldn't even go to a ball game until the second inning. Why? So he wouldn't have to stand for the National Anthem.

He was the laziest man in the church. "One of these days you'll die and they'll take you out to the cemetery and bury you; then you can rest all you want to," suggested the chairman of the nominating committee who couldn't enlist him for a job in his church.

"No," said the idle church member, "It'll just be my luck the day I die, it'll be resurrection morning the next day, and I'll *have* to get up!"

Down in a little country village, a guide was showing a city feller the advantages of the community. He finally came to a tall oak tree in the village square.

"Yonder," he said, "in the sheltering branches of that oak tree lies the laziest man in this community."

"Oh, come on," said the stranger charitably, "you may be too harsh in your judgment. After all, it's a hot day. What's the harm of taking a little nap?"

"Nap, heck!" snapped the guide. "Do you know how he got in the tree? Thirty years ago he laid his self down on an acorn!"

Discouraged Wife: "There was a broken lock on the front door. The only way I could get my husband to fix it was to tell him my mother was coming to visit!"

A man was driving down the road and saw a

fellow lying under a tree. He stopped and asked the man the way to a certain town. The man barely pointed a toe to the north.

"I'll declare," the driver said, "if you'll show me something lazier than that, I'll give you a dollar."

The man didn't even open his eyes as he spoke. "Roll me over," he said, "and put your dollar in my pocket."

The worst part of doing nothing is that you never have a day off.

Mom: "What are you doing to conserve energy?"
Son: "I take a nap every afternoon."

You know you are out of shape when walking your dog makes you wheeze so loudly that cars pull over when they hear you coming.

Marriage

The preacher encountered a woman at whose wedding he had officiated.

"And does your husband always live up to the promises made during his courtship days?" he asked.

"He sure does," she snapped. "In those days he kept saying he wasn't good enough for me, and he has been proving it ever since."

A man, after being married two years, went to the pastor and said, "Pastor, I'm in trouble—that woman you married me to."

The pastor said, "What's the trouble?"

"She is always wanting money—money—money, all the time."

The pastor asked, "What does she do with all the money you give her?"

"I don't know—I haven't given her any yet."

"How come you never married?" a man asked an old friend.

"I really don't know," replied the bachelor. "I've come close many times. Just yesterday I fell in love with a girl at first sight."

"Are you going to marry her?"

"No, I took a second look."

After a country wedding, the new bridegroom asked the preacher, "How much do I owe you?"

"Just as much as you think the girl's worth," replied the preacher.

The bridegroom handed the minister a dollar, which was accepted without comment. But the couple didn't leave and the preacher thought he might never get rid of them.

"Have I forgotten something?" asked the minister.

"Yes," said the young groom, "my change."

A little girl asked her mother, "Why do they rope off the aisle at a wedding? So the bridegroom can't get away?"

There was a rich oil man who was getting married and was nervous about it. He told the minister that the fee would be in proportion to the brevity of the service and that if he used a long service he wouldn't receive a cent.

When the wedding day came, the couple stood before the minister in the bride's home. The minister said to the man, "Take her?"; to the woman,

"Take him?" and then closed the ceremony by pronouncing, "Took."

He's been married to the same woman for twenty-eight years. Well, not really. After twenty-eight years of living with him, she's not quite the same woman.

The world is full of men who started out helping girls with their homework—and wound up doing their housework.

"I've just been to my husband's cremation," said the widow.

"Oh, you poor thing," cried the single lady sitting by her on the plane. "I'm so sorry for you."

"He was my fourth husband," confided the widow, "I've cremated them all."

At this the stranger burst into tears.

"Have I said something to upset you?" asked the widow anxiously.

"Oh, no," she answered, still sobbing, "but I was thinking how unjust the world is! I've never had one husband and you have had husbands to burn."

In some homes, the husband runs the show, but the wife writes the script.

A farmer called the doctor and stated that his wife had dislocated her jaw and couldn't talk.

"Doc, if you happen to be out this way in the next two or three months and have time, I wish you'd take a look at her."

Lots of people get divorces on the grounds of incompatibility. That means he has no income, and she has no patability.

Bachelor: An average male over 21 whom no average female has ever made a serious attempt to marry.

Man to a friend: "When is your sister thinking of getting married?"
Friend: "Constantly."

A couple had been going together for a long time. He just couldn't work up the courage to ask her to marry him. One night he couldn't think of anything to say so there was silence for a long, long, time. At last he cleared his throat.

"I'm a man of a few words," he said. "What about getting married?"

After another long wait, she looked up at him, "I'm a woman of few words," she said, "You talked me into it!"

Memory

Can you remember when today's "bare necessities" were considered "luxuries"?

The brilliant counsel was addressing a judge and was obviously extremely hostile to the cause being pleaded. Nevertheless, counsel persisted in his argument which was long, involved, and highly technical.

When he finally concluded, the judge said sneeringly, "This lawyer has spoken at great length and with a good deal of eloquence, and I know it must pain him when I say that I, for one, have been left as ignorant as ever."

Quick as a flash, counsel was on his feet retorting, "Ignorant—yes, judge, but surely a good deal better informed."

Question: "What do you think about the international crisis?"
Answer: "Good tractor."

A giraffe and an elephant were getting a drink of water out of a river when the elephant spotted a snapping turtle asleep on a rock. He walked over as quietly as he could, picked it up with his trunk, and hurled it across the river.

"Why did you do that?" asked the giraffe.

"Because," the elephant said, "I recognized that guy as the same turtle who took a nip at my trunk over fifty years ago out of this same river."

"What a memory!" exclaimed the giraffe.

"Yes," the elephant humbly said, "I call it TURTLE RECALL!"

Sign in a farmer's berry garden: "No Trespassing! This is not a strawberry shortcut!"

A minister went to see a couple. They offered him a glass of spirits. Said the minister, "Do you know who I am?"

"No," said the couple, "but if you remember where you live we'll take you home."

You're as young as you feel, until you tend to forget the things you never remembered very well.

A man was traveling across the country all by himself in a balloon. While passing over a farm he spotted a farmer bailing hay.

"Helloooo!" shouted the balloonist down to the farmer. "Where am I?"

The farmer looked up and shook his head. "You can't fool me, feller," he retorted. "You're right up there in that little basket."

He was fired because of illness and fatigue. His boss was sick and tired of him!

The town know-it-all met a young boy on the street and asked, "Son, do you go to school?"

"Sure I do," the boy answered.

"Do you study math and algebra?" the man asked.

"Sure," was the reply.

The man smiled. "Could you give me the answer to a simple little problem?"

The boy shrugged, "Sure, I guess I can."

"All right, here it is. I'm out in a boat twelve feet long, in water ten feet deep, and I am fifty feet from the bank. How old am I?"

The young boy studied for a minute and then said, "Forty-four."

"That's right," the man said, surprised. "But how did you figure it out?"

"It wasn't hard," the boy answered. "I know a half-witted friend who asks silly questions like that, and he's only twenty-two."

A reporter was interviewing an elderly gentleman. "Sir, can you remember the first girl you ever kissed?"

The man giggled and answered, "Son, I can't even remember the last girl I kissed."

Neighbors

Two farmers carried on a feud for years. One said to the other, "We better hurry this feud up, cuz they's building a freeway thru here next month!"

One morning a mailman had a package for Mrs. Godsey who lived in an apartment house. He blew his whistle several times and yelled the name "Godsey" before a voice from the top floor answered, "Yes?"

"Package for Mrs. Godsey," he said. "Will you please come down and sign for it?"

"What kind of package?" the voice asked.

"A large one," replied the mailman.

"Who does it come from?"

"From a Mr. Jones."

"From where?" persisted the lady.

"From California," he told her, in resigned tone. "Will you please come down and sign for it?"

"What's in the package?" she asked.

"I can't tell you, madam," the mailman hollered. "I don't know."

"You don't know, and can't tell me what's in the package?"

"No, Madam," he answered, losing all that was left of his temper. "I cannot!"

There was a pause. "Well," she finally said, "You'll have to come back tomorrow. Mrs. Godsey is not home."

In a small farm community, all the phones were on party lines and neighbors listened in for miles. Everyone was disturbed by the prolonged dry spell. One night old Hank, a shrewd cattle rancher, got a call from a buyer at the Stock Yards, "Understand you've got some steers to sell."

"Well now," dickered Hank, "I'm not sure I want to sell right now."

"Hank, for heaven's sake!" broke in an agonized voice from the party line, "you sell them steers! You know you ain't got no grass."

Old Age

Not only are children a great comfort in old age, but they help you get there sooner.

Old age is when you don't care where your wife goes as long as you don't have to go with her.

"Why do older people keep using candles on their birthday cakes?"
"Because they want to make light of their age."

Three men were discussing the fact that age was dulling their memory. The first said that he often went to the refrigerator, opened the door, but couldn't remember what he wanted.

The second man said, "I have found myself halfway up the stairs trying to decide whether I was going up or down."

The third man said, "I have a lot to be thankful for; my memory is sharp as ever." Then he knocked on wood three times and said, "Excuse me, someone must be at the door."

Old age is when you get winded just from opening the telephone directory.

A woman who lived far beyond her three score and ten years had been in the habit of having a birthday party each year. Her friends and relatives always remembered her with little gifts which were usually in the form of knickknacks for her house.

Finally, arriving at the age of ninety, the old lady was asked by a friend what she wanted for her birthday this year.

"Give me a kiss," she answered, "so I won't have to dust it."

It doesn't matter that you fall down as long as you pick up something from the floor while you're down there.

There's an eighty-year-old man who is as unconscious of his age as a twenty-year-old. One cold day he came in wet and muddy from the knees down.

"I wanted to cross the creek to see about the cow," he explained to his son-in-law. "I used to jump it clear and easy, but now every time I try

I land in the middle. Guess I just ain't noticed it getting wider."

An elderly man approached his doctor and said, "Doctor, I'm slowly going nuts over women. Is there any way to speed it up?"

The preacher said to a man he had just met. "How old are you?" To his surprise the man replied, "Ninety-five."

The preacher said, "You don't look like you're more than sixty years old. How do you account for holding your age so well and that great tan?"

The man said, "When my wife and I married we made an agreement. When one of us became angry, the other would just go outside and stay until he or she got in a good humor. I have spent most of my life out in the open."

After his speech at a civic organization, a very diplomatic speaker was approached by a little white-haired woman who told him how much she had enjoyed his talk.

"I take the liberty to speak to you," she said, "because you told us you love old ladies."

"I do, I do," was the gallant reply. "I also like them your age."

Old age is always fifteen years older than the speaker!

You are not getting old as long as:
Your fling is not flung,
Your song is not sung,
Your bell is not rung,
Your spring is not sprung,
Your fun is not done!

An old sportsman says that the declining years are those in which a man declines almost everything.

A ninety-year-old man got into a bitter argument with the town shoe cobbler over how a pair of shoes should be made.

"Now look," said the shoemaker, "you're past ninety, and there's no way you'll live long enough to wear out these shoes. And why are you so concerned about how they're made?"

The old timer looked sternly at the shoemaker and said, "Apparently you aren't aware that statistics prove very few people die after ninety years of age."

"The future is changing," stated a wise man with a twinkle in his eye. "It now gets here a lot quicker than it used to."

A man in a testimonial service at the church had found a good way to get rid of his troubles. "I'm ninety-six years old," he said, "and don't have an enemy in the world."

"That's wonderful," a deacon said. "How do you account for it?"

The old man chuckled. "Every one of 'em is dead."

As you grow older you can make a fool of yourself in a much more dignified manner.

Old Fashioned

Book salesman to farmer: "Better buy an encyclopedia now that your boy is going to school."
Farmer: "Nothing doing. Let him walk, same as I did!"

Daughter: "I never use a thimble when I sew."
Mother: "You better start using one—you'll get stuck without it!"

In a store an elderly man saw some socks that were priced two pairs for $1.98. He bought them.
"Two dollars and ten cents, please," the saleslady said.
"The sign says $1.98," he answered.
"The twelve cents is for tax," she explained.
"Well, never mind," he said, "I don't use tacks. I wear garters."

A woman farmer from way back in the hills walked eight miles to the general store.
"Hello, Jo," said the proprietor. "Tell me, are you still making the fires up there by rubbing stone and flint together?"
"Yep, we're still doing it. Why?"

"A new-fangled thing just came out. Something to make fires with. It's called matches."

"Matches? Never heard of 'em."

"I'll show you how they work. If you want a fire, you just do this," said the proprietor, taking a match and striking it on his pants.

"Well, that's all right, but it's no good for me," said Jo.

"Why not?"

"I can't walk eight miles every time I want a fire and borrow your pants."

Pigs

A farmer asked his neighbor why his sow was on the fence. He replied, "Because the young ones tickle."

A visitor to a small country town noticed that every morning a native would pass going north with a drove of razorback hogs. Then about sundown, every evening he would return.

One morning the visitor asked the native where he was going. He replied, "Over thar, tother side of the mountain."

"How far is it over there?"

"Three miles."

"Why do you take them over there?"

"To graze."

"Why don't you move over there?"

"What fur?"

"To save time!"

"Time! What's time to a hog?"

The three little pigs did time in the pen. Yuk!

Gene: "Where do you keep a herd of hogs in the city?"

Kay: "In a porking lot."

A farmer kept lifting his pig up to a tree to eat an apple growing there.

A passerby saw him doing this and said, "Why don't you take a bunch of apples and put them in a trough? It'll save time!"

"You dummy," sneered the farmer, "pigs don't care about time!"

A speeding car ran over one of the farmer's hogs.

"Don't worry," said the driver of the car. "I'll replace your hog."

"You can't," said the farmer. "You ain't fat enough."

Farmer: "Things are so rough at our farm that we had to take our pig to the pawn shop."

Friend: "I never heard of that."

Farmer: "Yes, they call it ham hock."

A weatherman asked one person: "Do you know what a ground hog is?"

The person answered: "Sure, it's sausage."

Health Inspector: "Don't you know it isn't healthy to let your hogs run around the house this way?"

Farmer: "Can't say that I do; we ain't lost nary a hog in fifteen years."

A farmer riding in a truck full of pigs with his wife said: "Quit complainin'; how many wives do you know that get to travel with their husbands?"

Jack: "What happened when the three little pigs finally got rid of the wolf?"

Jill: "They went hog-wild!"

A thrilled little boy came to school and told his teacher that his family had six little pigs.

The next morning the little boy was late to school and, remembering how thrilled he was, the teacher asked, "How are all those little pigs this morning?"

He beamed and said, "Just fine. How are all your folks?"

A thief holding a pig told the officer, "I wasn't stealin' him, deputy; I'm a'takin' him to lunch!"

Recipes

Mike: "Want to make a fortune?"
Jeff: "Yeah! How?"
Mike: "Buy a box of Cheerios and sell them as doughnut seeds."

Opossum Stew

Cut up 326 large opossums into small bite-size pieces. Add enough brown gravy to cover. Cook over gas fire in oven pot for about four weeks, maintaining 465 degrees.

Add three bushels of onions, twelve bushels of potatoes, two bushels of carrots. Season with lots of thyme, sage, and then salt and pepper to taste. Cook two more weeks.

This will serve 1,800 people. If more people are expected, two rabbits may be added. Add the rabbit only if necessary. Some people do not like hare in their stew!

A lady was baking oatmeal cookies. When the phone rang in the den, she had a batch in the oven. After a long conversation, she remembered her cookies and rushed into the kitchen to find it filled with smoke.

Quickly she removed the charred cookie sheets and sat down utterly depressed. Suddenly, she felt the soft hand of her three-year-old. "Don't feel bad, Mama," said the tiny voice, "that's the best-smelling smoke you ever made."

Mom: "If I cut two oranges and two bananas into ten pieces, what will I get?"
Son: "Fruit salad."

The officer-of-the-day stopped a mess orderly carrying a soup kettle out of the kitchen.

"Hey you!" he snapped. "Give me a taste of that." Obediently the orderly handed him a spoon and the officer tasted.

"Good grief, do you call that soup?" he roared.

"No, sir," replied the orderly, "I call that dirty dishwater!"

Question: "How many people does it take to make chocolate cookies?"
Answer: "It takes two—one to make the batter and the other to peel the M&Ms."

Kid: "I want a large malt."
Clerk: "Any special instructions?"

Kid: "No, I just want to be sure I get a fair shake."

A farmer was eating for the first time at a fashionable restaurant. The soup of the day was "different," to say the least.

"Waiter," he asked, "what do you call this stuff?"

"That's bean soup, sir," snapped the waiter haughtily.

"I don't care what it's been, what is it now?"

Relatives

"So you're not bothered anymore with relatives coming and staying?" asked a friend.

"No," he answered with satisfaction. "I borrow money from the rich ones and lend it to the poor ones. None of them ever come back."

A father was heard complaining that everytime he tried to call home that either his wife or the kids were on the phone. He said that even sea shells gave him a busy signal.

Cannibal

An inhabitant of several continents who lives on other people. In America, they're called "relatives."

I won't say she's ugly. But, when she got married—it took three of her relatives to give her away.

An uncle came for dinner and before leaving gave his nephew ten dollars. "Now be careful with that money," the uncle advised. "Remember the saying, 'A fool and his money are soon parted.'"

"Yes, Uncle," replied the boy, "but I want to thank you for parting with it just the same."

"I need a job, Senator," said the Senator's brother.

The Senator thought for a moment. Then he replied, "There aren't any jobs. But here's what I'll do. I'll get up a committee to investigate why there are no jobs, and you can be chairman."

"The country store manager keeps adding his sons to the firm's payroll."

"I guess a lot of people are upset about that!"

"Yes, he has been accused of putting on heirs!"

An outlaw is a person who kicks his in-law out.

The warden of one of the more advanced prisons began to feel sorry for one of the prisoners. On visitor's day, while most of the prisoners received relatives and friends, this man sat alone in his cell.

One visiting day, the warden called him into the office. "Don," he said kindly, "I notice you never have any callers. Don't you have any friends or family?"

"Oh sure," replied the man happily, "but they're all in here."

A fellow had two friends who had the same last name. The fellow asked the first if he was any relation to the second, to which he replied, "No, I have no relations of my own. My father was the last of his race."

Suspicion

Joe and Mike had jobs at a cotton mill. One morning the foreman came along and found Joe reading a letter to his co-worker.

"Hey," cried the foreman, "what kind of horse-play you two guys up to?"

"Mike got a letter from his girl friend," explained Joe, "but he can't read, so I'm readin' the letter for him."

"How come you got the cotton in your ears?"

"Mike don't want me to hear what his girlfriend wrote to him!"

Two traffic judges were driving home together at night when they were stopped by a motorcycle policeman. They were duly charged and, when their cases came up for hearing the next day, they agreed that each would leave the bench to have his case heard by the other.

The first went to trial, pleaded guilty and was promptly fined fifty dollars. When they changed places the second traffic judge, after pleading guilty, was rather shocked to receive a fine of one hundred dollars from his friend.

"That's a bit unfair," he whispered, "I only fined you half that amount."

"I know," was the reply, "but there is too much

of this sort of thing—this is the second case we've had today!"

A preacher stated in his sermon: "God doesn't strike people dead for lying in these modern times. It He did where would you be?"

A smile came over the faces in the congregation, but the preacher hadn't finished.

"I'll tell you where I'd be. I'd be right here preaching to an empty church."

The farmer fleeced his own sheep and carried the wool to the mill.

On one occasion, he came to a large lake around which he usually walked with his heavy load. However, it being winter, the lake was frozen. He figured he could save a lot of time by pulling his load straight over the frozen pond on a sled.

But the owner of the pond ran out of his house screaming, "You can't pull the wool over my ice!"

"If you live here, you'll never be bothered by earthquakes," the real estate agent explained *faultlessly*.

A farmer was paying his first visit to a large city.

A panhandler walked up to him on a downtown street and asked, "Would you give me a dollar for a sandwich?"

"I don't know," said the farmer, "lemme see the sandwich."

You are misinformed if you suspect that when you go into a bank and look around, they turn off the hidden camera.

As a motorist drove away from a farmer's orchard he shouted, "We picked some of your apples. We didn't think you'd mind."

"Not at all," yelled the farmer after them. "I picked some of your car's tools from the trunk. I didn't think you'd mind, either."

Did you hear about the farmer who ran a steamroller across his fields because he wanted to sell mashed potatoes?

Tact

A sick man lived several miles out of town. "Doctor," he said, "isn't it pretty far out of your way to visit me here?"

"It's not too bad," the doctor said. "I have another patient right down the road, so I'm able to kill two birds with one stone."

Some people cause happiness wherever they go; others, whenever they go.

"Son, I'll give you a dime if you can tell me where God is," the atheist told a small boy.

The boy's polite reply was, "I'll give you a quarter if you can tell me where he isn't!"

A woman went to the police station to get help in finding her husband who had disappeared.

"I'll do my best," the policeman said. "Give me a description."

But she couldn't give him a description that was helpful.

"Well, do you have a picture?" the policeman asked.

"Yes, right here in my purse." She took it out and handed it to the policeman.

He studied it a minute and then sighed. "Lady, why in the world do you want to find him?"

"I would like to come right over and make plans for the burial of my wife!"

"Your wife?" gasped the funeral director, "didn't we bury her just two years ago?"

"You don't understand. I married again."

"Well, congratulations!"

"Does your husband ever talk to himself?" one woman asked another.

"Yes, the poor dear, but he doesn't mean to. He thinks I'm listening."

A total stranger walked up to a woman on the street, hugged her, kissed her, and said, "You are the most beautiful woman in the world."

They arrested him and accused him of assault and flattery.

The quickest way to exit an antique shop is to ask, "What's new?"

"You seem to have a speech peculiarity," a man said to the stuttering ball player.

"S-s-s-ure," the stutterer answered. "Don't you have any p-p-p-peculiarities?"

The other man shook his head. "Not that I know of."

"S-s-sure you do," the stutterer insisted. "Which hand do you stir your coffee with?"

The man thought a minute. "My right hand," he answered.

"There now," the stutterer beamed. "I knew you were p-p-peculiar. I s-s-stir mine with a sp-sp-spoon."

Overheard by a nurse: "Of course, I wear a mask during my surgery. That way, they're never sure of the one to blame."

Ted: "I can't be as dumb as I look."
Charles: "You're right, nobody could be!"

Weather

One day it rained hard, and the Sunday School teacher announced, "Tickets for Noah's Ark will go on sale after class."

> No dashing rain can make us stay
>   When we have tickets for a play;
> But if a drop the walk besmirch,
>   It is too wet to go to church!

One hot summer day a minister met a woman he hadn't seen for years. He asked, "How is your husband standing the heat?" The minister didn't know he had been dead for two years!

A tornado hit a farm and did $20,000 worth of improvements.

A minister from a large city church was the guest preacher at a rural church. They asked him to pray for rain. He did pray, and the rain came in floods and destroyed some of the crops.

One deacon remarked to another, "This comes

from making such a request of a minister who isn't acquainted with agriculture."

Summer is the time when it's too hot to do the things it was too cold to do in the winter.

A four-year-old asked, "Why does it rain, Daddy?"

"To make the flowers grow," said the father, "also the grass and the trees."

"So why does it rain on the sidewalk?"

A family with four small boys had moved to California from Oklahoma. When earthquake warnings were given, the mother was terrified. She sent the boys back to Oklahoma to visit their relatives.

On the third day she received a phone call: "Come get the boys and send us the earthquake!"

There was this fellow who opposed Daylight Saving Time on the premise that the extra hour would burn the grass.

An elderly farmer was finishing his haying one

Sunday morning as the pastor of the local church drove by.

"Brother," the minister lectured him, "Don't you know that the Creator made the world in six days and rested on the seventh?"

"Yes," said the old farmer, as he looked uneasily at the rain clouds in the West. "I know all about that, but He got done and I didn't."

Wisecracks

Did you hear about the medical student who invented an artificial appendix?

A traveling salesman asked the farmer why the train station was so far from town. The farmer replied, "I guess because they wanted to put it near the tracks."

"My work's *dun*," said the bill collector.

"My teenage son obeys me perfectly."
"Amazing. How do you do it?"
"I tell him to do as he pleases."

When the condemned criminal was asked what style of death he wanted, he replied: "If it's all the same, I'll take old age."

A vote was taken in the church and the moderator said, "Let's make it unanimous."
A cantankerous church member retorted,

"There ain't nothin' going to be unanimous as long as I'm a member of this church."

Query: Is life worth living?
Answer: Depends on the liver.

"How can you be so stupid?"
"Well, it sure ain't something you just pick up!"

"What can you say about a blacksmith who is making hardware for a bathroom?"
"He's forging ahead."

What can't be held for ten minutes although it's light as a feather?
Answer: Your breath.

"A man worked for years and finally invented the broom."
"Then what happened?"
"He was so tired he went to *sweep.*"

A tourist, going through a small town, asked a

local minister: "Say, preacher, have any big men ever been born in this little town?"

The minister, the last man on earth to hurt anybody's feelings, couldn't resist saying, "I am afraid not, sir. The best we ever produce are babies."

Bill: "What do you get at a corn auction?"
Cindy: "You get auction-ears."

Mother: "Why don't you go out and play hide-and-seek?"
Son: "Because nobody will come to find me!"

Question: "Who was the first man to wear an Arrow shirt?"
Answer: "General Custer."

A man sat in the pew, scratching and scratching. The preacher stopped his sermon and asked, "Why are you scratching like that?"

Said the man, " 'Cause I'm the only one who knows where I itch."

Jim: "What do they call a farm where they raise chimpanzees?"

Jack: "A Monkey Ranch." Get it?

Specialist:

A man who has discovered which of his talents will bring in the most money

He's so dumb he thinks Gatorade is welfare for crocodiles.

A small-town jail carried a sign over the door: "Amoeba."

When asked why, the sheriff explained, "Because our jail has just one cell!"

Two farmers visited the city for the first time and examined, with interest, the cement sidewalks.

"You can't hardly blame the city people for not farming," one of them said. "The ground's too hard for plowin'."

When you are up to your nose in trouble, keep your mouth shut.

Did you hear about the turtle that wore people-neck sweaters?

That man is so cheap! You know what he does to save haircut money? He freezes his hair and then just breaks them off!"

Bill: "Which travels faster, heat or cold?"
Joe: "Heat!"
Bill: "Why?"
Joe: "Because you can always catch cold."

Question: How do you get rid of an extra T?
Answer: Throw it in depot.

Leftover Miscellaneous

There was a fellow who always used some Scripture to justify what he did. One day a horse trader came through the country and this guy traded him a horse that had hives.

After the trader went on his way, the wife said to her husband, "Now, I know you always find Scripture to justify what you do. Just what Scripture will you use to justify trading that sick horse to the man who came by?"

"He was a stranger and I took him in," he replied.

Farm Taxes

Tax his cow,
    tax his goat,
Tax his pants,
    tax his coat,
Tax his crops,
    tax his work,
Tax his tie,
    tax his shirt,
Tax his chew,
    tax his smoke;
Teach him taxes
    are no joke.

Tax his tractor,
  tax his mule,
Teach him taxes
  are a rule,
Tax his oil,
  tax his gas,
Tax his notes,
  tax his cash;
Tax him good
  and let him know—
After taxes
  he has no dough.
If he hollers,
  tax him more;
Tax him 'til
  he's good and sore.
Tax his coffin,
  tax his grave,
Tax the sod
  in which he lays.
Put these words
  upon his tomb:
"Taxes drove me
  to my doom."
And after he's gone
  he can't relax;
They'll still be after
  Inheritance Tax!

Bob: "I just bought a new book on lawn care."
Bill: "Why?"
Bob: "'Cause I want to be a good weeder."

Looking for bargains? Go where the auction is!

Gardener to store owner: "Do you have something that will cause crab grass a very slow and painful death?"

Wouldn't the world be a richer place if the housefly, which lays 20,000 eggs a season, could be crossed with a hen?

This is a day in which everybody knows the troubles we've got, but nobody knows what to do about them.

Question: What animals failed to come to Noah's Ark in pairs?
Answer: Worms. They came in apples.

At a farm auction, a man lost his wallet with

$300 in it. He rushed to the front and hollered an offer of a seventy-five-dollar reward.

"I'll give $100" said one bidder. "$150" came from another. "$200" said a third. That wallet finally brought $1000!

City man to farmer: "How far is it to Clinton, if I keep straight on?"

Reply: "Well, if you're a goin' to keep straight on, it's about 25,000 miles, but if you turn 'round t'other way it's about half a mile!"

During a break on a building project a construction worker approached a fellow worker. "I hear the boys is gonna' strike."

"What for?" asked the friend.

"Shorter hours."

"Good for them, I always did think sixty minutes was too long for an hour."

A duck walks into a store and says to a clerk, "I'd like some lipstick, please."

The clerk looks a little aghast at a duck asking for lipstick, but he goes and gets a tube, hands it to the duck, and say's "That's $2.98."

The duck replied, "Oh, just put it on my bill!"

Teacher: "Spell mouse."
Student: "M-o-u-s."
Teacher: "But what's at the end of it?"
Student: "A tail."

Did you hear about the Gardener's Union that passed out leaflets at its meeting?